IOWA

Copyright © 1986 Raintree Publishers Limited Partnership

A Turner Educational Services, Inc. book. Based on the Portrait
of America television series created by R.E. (Ted) Turner.

Library of Congress Number: 85-12169

345678910   949392919089

Library of Congress Cataloging in Publication Data

Thompson, Kathleen.
   Iowa.

   (Portrait of America)
   "A Turner book."
   Summary: Discusses the history, economy, culture,
and future of Iowa. Also includes a state
chronology, pertinent statistics, and maps.
   1. Iowa—Juvenile literature. [1. Iowa]
I. Title. II. Series: Thompson, Kathleen. Portrait of
America.
F621.3.T46   1985   977.7   85-12169
ISBN 0-86514-431-1 (lib. bdg.)
ISBN 0-86514-506-7 (softcover)

Cover Photo: Charlton Photos

Portrait of AMERICA

IOWA

Kathleen Thompson

A TURNER BOOK
RAINTREE PUBLISHERS

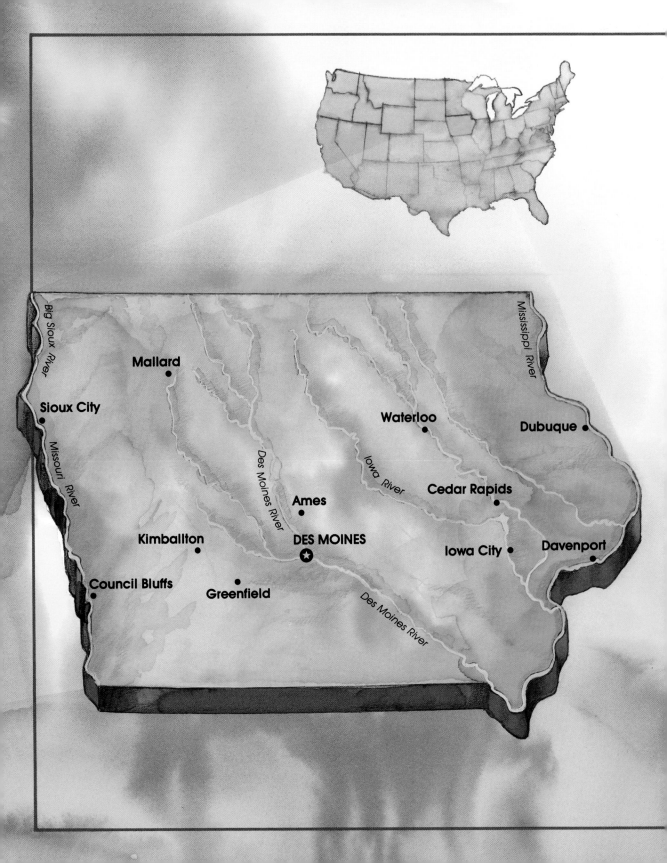

Big Sioux River

Mississippi River

Missouri River

Mallard

Sioux City

Waterloo

Dubuque

Des Moines River

Iowa River

Cedar Rapids

Ames

Kimballton

DES MOINES

Iowa City

Davenport

Council Bluffs

Greenfield

Des Moines River

CONTENTS

Introduction   7

In the Middle of the Middle West   8
   Doc and Dan   20

Iowa Feeds the World   22
   Neighbors   28
   Grant Wood   30

Art Grows in Iowa   34
   Getting Your Name in the Paper   38

A Slow Move into the Future   42
   Important Historical Events in Iowa   45
   Iowa Almanac   46
   Places to Visit/Annual Events   47
   Map of Iowa Counties   48
   Index   49

Introduction

Iowa, the Hawkeye State.

"I have been around to the cities and I have been around the country and (here) it's nice and slow all year. Nobody botherin' ya."

Iowa: black earth, corn, schools, neighbors, and hogs.

"My dad had a farm for me when I started up—to help me get started. And now I'm just trying to get my boys started farming. That's the way out here, the way people are—that it goes from one generation down to the next."

Iowa is the old American dream. It is the way America was supposed to be. It's farmers working hard to bring fine crops out of rich soil. It's neighbors working together and taking care of each other. It's close families and good schools and all the traditional values.

But is there something behind the almost mythical surface of life in Iowa? Can the life of nineteenth-century America survive in the world of the twentieth century?

In the Middle
of the Middle West

Long ago, there was a country that people called paradise on earth. Between the Tigris and Euphrates rivers, Mesopotamia flourished as the most fertile spot on earth. The soil was unbelievable in its richness. The climate was mild. It was a vast garden in the Middle East.

Far from that ancient land, across the Atlantic Ocean, glaciers formed another paradise. Between the Missouri and Mississippi rivers, rich top soil was deposited by melting ice sheets. The climate was perfect for growing things. It was—and it is—a vast garden in the American Midwest.

The state of Iowa may be the most fertile spot on earth.

In the days of Mesopotamia, Iowa was the home of a people we call the Mound Builders. What they called them-

A typical Iowa farm, with corn in the foreground.

selves is lost in time. A thousand years ago they lived, farmed, hunted, and fought on the land between America's two great rivers. They also built long mounds of earth where they buried their dead. Much of what we know about these ancient Indians we have learned from the tools and weapons they buried in the mounds.

After the Mound Builders came other tribes. To the east, near the Mississippi, were the Illinois, Iowa, Miami, and Ottawa Indians. To the west, along the banks of the Missouri, lived the Omaha, Oto and Missouri Indians. Others came later, forced westward by the white man.

The first Europeans to enter the area were scarcely noticed by the inhabitants. They were French explorers, Louis Joliet and Father Jacques Marquette. They did not stay, and it was a long time before anyone followed them onto Indian land.

But, unknown to the woodland and plains Indians who lived in Iowa, their land was being claimed by the French. In 1682, Robert Cavelier, Sieur de la Salle, traveled down the Missis-sippi River and claimed the entire Mississippi Valley for his country. Iowa was part of this area that La Salle called Louisiana.

Over the next hundred years, a few Europeans wandered into Iowa. But they were not settlers. They were mostly traders and missionaries. For the most part, they did not disturb the Indians, and the Indians did not bother them.

One man, Nicholas Perrot, taught the Miami Indians how to mine for lead. Another, Julien Dubuque, was allowed by the

Below is an aerial view of mounds at Iowa City and a close-up view of a mound near Boone.

This map shows how the United States expanded between 1783 and 1853.

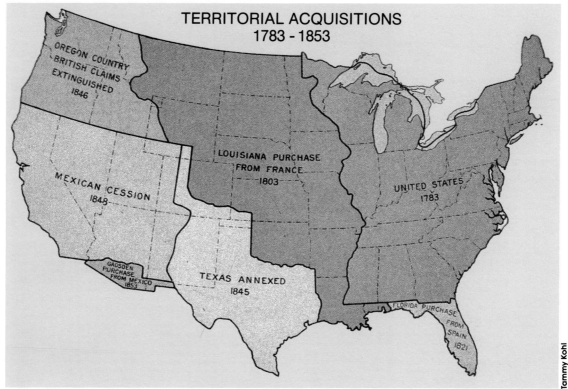

TERRITORIAL ACQUISITIONS
1783 - 1853

OREGON COUNTRY
BRITISH CLAIMS
EXTINGUISHED
1846

LOUISIANA PURCHASE
FROM FRANCE
1803

UNITED STATES
1783

MEXICAN CESSION
1848

GADSDEN
PURCHASE
FROM MEXICO
1853

TEXAS ANNEXED
1845

FLORIDA PURCHASE
FROM
SPAIN
1821

Tammy Kohl

Fox Indians to mine for lead himself. He came into the area in 1788 and is considered the first white settler.

In the meantime, the European countries were playing political games with the Mississippi Valley. In 1762, France gave Spain the area west of the river. Then, in 1800 Spain gave it back. Three years later, Napoleon sold the whole region to the United States in order to raise money for a war in Santo Domingo.

Thomas Jefferson, who was President of the United States at the time, was really only trying to buy New Orleans and Florida. But when he offered ten million dollars for the two, Napoleon offered to throw in the whole Louisiana area for another five million dollars. It was an offer Jefferson couldn't refuse. The Louisiana Purchase more than doubled the size of the United States at a cost of about four cents an acre.

Having bought this enormous

On the right is a painting of the Sauk Indian chief Black Hawk. On the right-hand page is a statue of Louis Joliet. He and Father Jacques Marquette were the first Europeans to enter Iowa.

parcel of land, Jefferson decided to look it over. So he sent Meriwether Lewis and William Clark out to explore. Guided by the sixteen-year-old Shoshone Indian girl Sacagawea, Lewis and Clark made it all the way to the Pacific Ocean. On their way through Iowa, a member of their group died and was buried near what is now Sioux City.

Another American explorer, Zebulon Pike, passed through the area a few years later. He was exploring the Mississippi River and visited Dubuque's settlement.

Iowa was still Indian land in 1812 when Congress declared it part of the Territory of Missouri. There were trading posts in the area now, set up by large fur companies. But they traded peacefully with the Indians. In 1821, Missouri became a state. Iowa became part of a large area of unorganized territory.

White settlers were still being kept out of Iowa, but more Indians were being pushed in. The Sauk and Fox Indians, who had lived in Illinois, were forced out to make room for more white Americans. But they did not go peacefully.

Chief Black Hawk, of the Sauk Indians, fought to stay in Illinois. The war that broke out was called the Black Hawk War. In that war, a young Illinois rail splitter named Abraham Lincoln led a group of state militia. His militiamen never saw battle, but Lincoln discovered that he was a born leader.

In the end, Black Hawk was defeated. The treaty that ended the war opened a small part of Iowa to white settlement for the first time. That fifty-mile strip

13

of land along the Mississippi River was called the Black Hawk Purchase. The area included some of the lead-rich land that Dubuque had mined and Pike had visited.

The Black Hawk Purchase was first attached to the Territory of Michigan. Then, in 1836, Congress created the Territory of Wisconsin and included the Black Hawk Purchase in that. Then, in 1838, Congress separated the land west of the Mississippi from the Wisconsin Ter-

ritory. A month later, the Territory of Iowa came into being.

The Territory of Iowa included a lot more than the present state of Iowa. Parts of Minnesota and North and South Dakota were in the package. Robert Lucas was named governor of the territory and he spent the next few years trying to turn Iowa into a state.

At first, the people living in Iowa didn't want any part of statehood. They had a very simple reason. So long as they were

a territory, government officials were paid by the federal government. When they became a state, the people would have to start paying those salaries themselves, out of their own taxes.

Finally, in 1844, the people of Iowa decided to apply for statehood. But they were turned down. Congress didn't like the boundaries they proposed for their new state. Then, when Congress suggested a set of boundaries, the people of Iowa turned them down. In 1846, an

agreement was reached and Iowa became a state on December 28. The first constitution was adopted eleven years later, in 1857.

All this time, settlers had been pushing farther and farther into Indian land. This land had belonged to the Indians for centuries. And it had been guaranteed to them by treaties with the United States government. In the same year that the Iowa constitution was adopted, a group of Sioux Indians attacked white settlers in western Iowa.

But the settlers could not be stopped. The Indians were killed or pushed farther west.

Just fifteen years after Iowa became the twenty-ninth state, the Civil War began. As a state, Iowa was against slavery. Iowa sent a higher percentage of its population to fight for the Union than any other state.

A few years after the war ended, the railroad came to Iowa. Now, farmers could ship their products easily to other parts of the country. Iowa was quickly becoming one of the states that fed the nation. But the railroad and the farmers ran into trouble. The railroads were charging higher prices to carry the goods than the farmers thought were fair. The farmers decided to do something about it.

Many American farmers belonged to a national organization called the Grange. One of the purposes of the Grange was to protect farmers' rights. In 1873, Iowa members of the Grange voted together and gained control of the state legislature. In 1874, the state legislature passed laws that limited rates the railroads could charge farmers. Four years later, the railroads managed to get these laws repealed. Finally, the state created a commission to work on the problem. They came up with rates that both the farmers and the railroads approved.

About the same time, something was happening that would change the way Iowa looked. On the Mississippi River, steamboats started moving big shipments of logs down from the lumbering states of Wisconsin

Iowa State Historial Dept. State Historical Society

Portrait of America

At the left is a present-day barn in Iowa. At the far left is a nineteenth-century photograph of logging on the Mississippi River.

and Minnesota. The farmers who had been living in cabins made of sod now built wooden houses. These pretty frame farmhouses became a permanent part of the Iowa landscape.

As Iowa entered the twentieth century, some important things began to change. Helped by the railroads, and new dams to provide power, industry moved into the state for the first time. Iowa was still almost entirely a farming state, but it was the

Iowa Development Commission

18

The drawing above depicts the kind of sod house that was on many farms until the late 1800s, when Iowa was almost totally agricultural. Today there is a lot of industry in Iowa—typified by the steel worker at the left.

beginning of a balance between agriculture and manufacturing that would later give Iowa a very stable economy.

The First World War came and with it came some changes that caused a lot of hardship in Iowa. Farmland became very valuable but, far from helping the farmers, this rise in the price of land made it very difficult for farmers to add to their farms. Many of them went far into debt. When the Great Depression came in 1929, farmers were unable to pay the mortgages they had taken out to borrow money for buying land. Six years later, more than half of Iowa's farmers had lost their farms.

Again, the farmers organized. They formed cooperatives so that they could pool their money to buy supplies. They also sold their crops together through the cooperatives. These organizations helped many Iowa farmers to keep their land. And better days were coming.

World War II created a large demand for farm products. That included Iowa's corn and hogs. Farmers began to make money again. After the war, industry started to move into the state in a big way. Most of it was directly related to agriculture. But it meant that a lot of people went from plowing the fields to making the plows. By 1960, more Iowans lived in urban than in rural areas.

Today, Iowa has reached the balance between industry and agriculture that it has been moving toward since the beginning of the century.

Below is veterinarian Doc Nesheim

Iowa State University

Doc and Dan

"Say, I got ahold of Arnold. We're going to stop in there now and treat a pneumonia. Would you get ahold of Gary Travis? He wanted me to kind of stop and look at his calves out in the pasture. See if he'd be around there in about a half hour."

Doc Nesheim is the vet from Mallard. He drives around from farm to farm in a pickup with a CB radio. He's a big man with a dry sense of humor and a feeling for the people he works with as well as for the animals he treats.

Doc grew up on a farm and went to veterinary school at Iowa State in Ames.

Dan Vonnahme is an old friend of Doc's. Dan raises hogs.

"Dan is one of my prized clients because he's kind of grown up with me and I've grown up with him. We started out with no money, and we worked without borrowing too much. And right now he's one of my more successful

Portrait of America

hog people. I feel that probably I've kind of added to the operation."

When Doc goes to vaccinate Dan's hogs, he manages to get in a jab or two at Dan.

"You notice as you travel around that the animals act a lot like their owner. These happen to be wild."

Well, Dan may not be as wild as his hogs, but he is a bit of a maverick. A lot of farmers in Iowa raise their hogs in buildings where the climate is controlled and the hogs don't have much room to move around. They say the hogs get fatter on less feed that way and it saves a lot of work. Dan doesn't think much of the method.

"When you never had anything when you started, well, you start with what you have and go from there. I'm not a confinement lover. I feel the best hogs are raised right out there in the dirt the way they were fifty years ago. I know people disagree with me, but I still maintain that that's the best way to raise hogs. 'Cause I don't believe a sow or a hog, a pig of any sort should live in something that costs more than what I live in."

Dan raises good hogs. Doc keeps them healthy. It's a good partnership and a good friendship.

Iowa Feeds the World

There's a Paul Bunyan story that could have been told about Iowa.

It seems that one day Paul planted a kernel of corn just to see whether the land was good for growing things. Within minutes, the corn had grown so high that Paul was worried it would poke a hole in the sky. So he sent one of his men climbing up the cornstalk to chop off the top. But the corn grew faster than the man could climb and he couldn't get down. So Paul loaded up a shotgun with biscuits and shot them up to feed his friend while he figured out how to get him down. Finally, Paul took a railroad track and wound it around the cornstalk. As the corn continued to grow, the metal cut into the stalk and it started to fall. Paul's friend jumped down and Paul decided that the land was good enough.

Maybe the farmland in Iowa isn't quite that fertile, but it's close. Deep layers of dark topsoil cover most of the state. In fact, 95 percent of the land in Iowa is farmable.

It's not surprising then that Iowa's economy is based on agriculture. Even most of the manufacturing is directly related to farming. But there is a balance.

About 50 percent of the value of goods produced in Iowa comes from manufacturing. About 49 percent comes from agriculture.

Nonelectric machinery is the biggest Iowa industry. Most of that machinery is farm equipment. Iowa's largest employer is the John Deere Company, which makes tractors, harvesters, combines, and other farm machinery.

The second largest area of manufacturing is food processing. Factories in Iowa's cities take goods from the farms and process them before they are shipped across the country and around the world. There are large meat-packing plants for hogs and cattle. Corn is turned into corn oil, cornstarch, corn

Iowa State University

Iowa's two largest industries are nonelectric machinery (right) and food processing, which includes meat packing (above).

sugar, and glucose. There are cereal mills and a large popcorn plant. In other plants, milk from dairy farms is pasteurized, homogenized, and packaged, or made into other dairy products. There are other industries in Iowa, but these are the largest.

And then there is agriculture.

It's hard to get a picture of just how much food is produced on Iowa farms. Iowa is second only to Texas in the production of beef cattle. It is number one in the nation in hogs, producing about one-fourth of the nation's total. Each year, it is either number one or number two in corn, and the same is true for soybeans. It produces about 18 percent of all the nation's corn and about 14 percent of the nation's soybeans.

The largest source of farm income in Iowa is beef cattle. They graze on Iowa grasslands and are also fed Iowa corn.

Next to beef as a moneymaker are hogs. Iowa farmers call them mortgage lifters. You can always make money on hogs. Other livestock raised on Iowa farms include dairy cattle, chickens, turkeys, sheep, and horses.

The two biggest Iowa crops are soybeans and corn. Soybeans are number one. Iowa farms grow about 291 million bushels of soybeans every year. Though corn is less valuable, there is

John Deere

Iowa is regarded as the most literate state in the country.

more of it. Iowa produces one and one-quarter *billion* bushels of corn every year. Most of that corn is fed to livestock.

Iowa farms also produce oats, hay, alfalfa, red clover, flaxseed, rye, and wheat. Fruits and vegetables are a smaller part of the produce grown in the state.

Altogether, there are 119,000 farms in Iowa. The balance between agriculture and industry is important to Iowa. When farming isn't producing much income, industry can usually make up for it. When industry goes through a slow period, Iowa relies on its farms.

There's a third partner in the Iowa story. Whether you're talking to a farmer or a manufacturer, you're likely to hear about the Iowa educational system.

They say you can't drive for fifty miles anyplace in Iowa without coming across a college or a university. That may be a bit of an exaggeration, but Iowans are understandably proud of their schools. Recent surveys have

Part of a school in Newton, Iowa, was built with private funds so that taxes would not have to be raised.

named Iowa as the most literate state in the country. Iowa produces more Ph.D.'s per capita than any other state and more high school graduates. A recent governor was asked what he was proudest of having achieved during his time in office. He pointed out that, during his fourteen years in the statehouse, Iowa had spent $200 million to expand the state's facilities for higher education. In Newton, a public school was built on private donations at a time when the town needed a school and didn't want to raise taxes.

Iowa's schools affect both agriculture and industry. Many Iowa farmers have been educated in modern methods of farming at the agricultural colleges. Much important agricultural research is done in Iowa universities. And the schools also produce trained workers for industry.

These three—agriculture, industry, and education—work together to make Iowa work.

Neighbors

"You do what you have to do. I've always been a fairly calm, take-things-as-it-comes person. I find a lot of comfort in my religion and my faith. Just pray, take one day at a time, and just be able to cope with it. And so far, I've really been able to. I have had help from above. I've had a lot of help from friends. It's just like they say—one day at a time."

Cheryl MacVey has needed all the calm—and all the help—she could get lately. Her husband Denny had to go down to Virginia to have a heart transplant. Things have been pretty hard for the whole MacVey family. But they have neighbors, and that helps. For one thing, the community had a pork patty dinner to raise money for the MacVeys.

"To us it just awesome. When we found out how many people were there and how much money was raised, we just couldn't believe it. And I think, like Denny and I both said, it wasn't so much that we got the money. It was the fact that everybody was thinking about us and helped us out. And we knew how many people really liked us back here. You know, it just lifted our spirits a lot."

The dinner was just one of the ways the neighbors helped out. They also came in to make sure the farm work got done. Hogs and crops don't wait for heart transplants or anything else.

"It's very comforting to know that things can be carried on without you for a while and that they're keeping things intact. They're keeping everything together for us. . . . It just comes so natural for them to come over and say, 'We'll do this for you and we'll do that, and we'll feed the hogs and put in the crops, take them out, whatever you need.' We just went to Tom 'cause he's done our chores for us before and said, 'Would you look after the hogs? Denny has to go to the hospital.' He said. 'Sure.'"

Tom Eberle is one of the neighbors. He doesn't think that what he and the others are doing is special. That's just the way things are in Iowa.

"I know the neighbors would come into my place just like I've come here. And the other neighbors have just all helped. That's just the way it's always been in this area. Oh, you worry about the weather and all the conditions—the big gambles, I guess you could call them. . . . But as far as me worrying about getting my crops in—if I'm sick or something, I know that there is somebody that will take over."

When you live in the country, where things are never easy and are sometimes very hard, you just help each other. That's all.

Iowa State University

Portrait of America

29

Grant Wood

"The depression with its farm strikes has emphasized for us all the fact that the farmer is basic in the economics of the country . . . an individual . . . capable of thinking and feeling . . . and not an oaf."

When Grant Wood said that, he was putting into words what he had put on canvas a hundred times.

Born in Cedar Rapids, Grant Wood grew up to become one of America's finest painters. He painted the world, and the peo-

At the left is the house that Grant Wood used in his painting **American Gothic.** *On the left-hand page is Esther Armstrong. She is also shown below with her husband, Robert, in front of a humorous version of Wood's painting.*

ple, around him. Though his paintings, at first glance, seem realistic, they are actually beautifully stylized. He exaggerated the almost geometric quality of carefully laid out fields. The people in his landscapes recall the figures in old Scandinavian folk art. He painted not only what his eyes saw, but what his heart and mind saw in the life of Iowa.

Esther Armstrong remembers talking to Wood about the new home he was going to help her design.

"He said that art should be indigenous, and I said to him, 'Do you think there is an indigenous Iowa architecture?' And he said, 'Oh, definitely there is. I will show it to you'."

And he did show it, not only to Esther Armstrong, but to everyone who looks at his painting. He showed the graceful frame houses that were built when lumber first came down the Mississippi from the north woods. He painted the clean lines of houses that are beautiful because they were built simply, to be lived in.

"He was a very fine artist, but he had the common touch. And he understood

These are two paintings by Grant Wood: a self-portrait (above) and Woman with Plant *(right-hand page.)*

people, and he was very considerate of people's thoughts. . . . Grant would take into consideration what the public thought about things.''

Grant Wood did have the common touch. His paintings stir something like recognition in us. It may be that we have never seen an Iowa farm, but a sense of familiarity is there. Perhaps that's because Wood painted the idea as well as the reality.

At the same time, Wood's paintings have an edge to them. They show great affection for their subjects but no sentimentality. They are not the sweet and pretty paintings of greeting cards. They are filled with humor and intelligence.

''This is a picture of Grant's mother, and I think it's really a very wonderful picture. I like it even better than Whistler's Mother, *and I think probably it's more notable. Mrs. Wood lived with Grant and he took care of her and she took care of him. She loved plants and I do, too. She gave me slips of all of these plants. This one here on the table is a descendant of the Sansevieria that she gave me. People call it mother-in-law's tongue or snake plant or something like that.''*

That's Grant Wood. He painted his mother with great love and affection and a pot of snake plant in her hands.

33

Art Grows in Iowa

For almost two centuries, American theater produced melodramas, sentimental comedies, vaudeville routines, musical extravaganzas, and European plays. What it did not produce was an important playwright. There seemed to be no room on the American stage for serious American drama.

And then, out of the heart of the country came a woman named Susan Glaspell. Many people have called her the first playwright in this country to write genuine dramatic literature.

Susan Glaspell was from Iowa. She wrote about people who lived on farms and spoke a bare, unemotional language, people who were better at hiding their feelings than showing them. Like her fellow Iowan, Grant Wood, she had affection for her subjects, but there was an edge to it. She went below the surface by viewing the surface with a clear, honest eye.

Susan Glaspell and Grant Wood are good examples of Iowa artists. The culture in this midwestern state does not encourage the wildly experimental. It brings out a kind of creativity that remains in touch with its roots.

At the University of Iowa, one of the most famous writers' workshops in the world cultivates the talents of writers like Flannery O'Connor, John Irving, and W.D. Snodgrass. The workshop reflects an Iowa attitude that talent, like corn, will grow better if it is nurtured. Art is not an accident.

The art of Iowa is strong because it is firmly rooted in the life of the people.

Musicians like Glenn Miller and Meredith Willson, the composer of *The Music Man,* made good music that was well loved by the people—who also take

Shown above is playwright Susan Glaspell. At the lower right is the original Glenn Miller band. Above, on the right-hand page, is the National Hot Air Ballon Race.

their recreation seriously. Yearly recreation events include jazz festivals, rodeos, bicycle races, and a nationwide hot-air balloon race.

Getting Your Name in the Paper

"My brother Ed and I are very much alike in many ways. He is smarter than I am—always was—got better grades, could write better than I could. Some days—about every other day—I think he was smarter also in what he decided to do. That was to be a country editor."

Hugh Sidey has been the White House correspondent for *Time* magazine for twenty-six years. His brother Ed publishes the *Adair County Free Press* in Greenfield, Iowa. A small town newspaper is like no other kind of newspaper, and Ed Sidey realizes it.

"One of the functions, I think, of a small town newspaper is to give everyone a spot in the news. It's the philosophy that—oh, my brother once was talking to Hubert Humphrey when he was a candidate and he said, 'The problem in the inner city is that people can be born and live and get married and die and never once have their names in the paper. . . .' So we put their names in when they are born, in our Stork Notes, and we run a big, long story when they are married, and we put a story on the front page when they die."

Adair County Free Press

Ed Sidey does some of his investigative reporting at the Ideal Cafe at nine-thirty every morning. Somebody from the paper is there at just about every special event in town. And, of course, Ed covers the county courthouse.

"We make a more or less deliberate effort to downplay crime news, although we do have a policy that it must go in. That is always an editor's problem: the person that gets picked up for drunk driving and doesn't want it in the paper

On the left is the building where Ed Sidey publishes the **Adair County Free Press**. *His brother Hugh is at the right.*

Below is Ed Sidey. On the right is a scene of one of the events that Ed normally covers—the Adair County Fair.

and comes to you and says, 'Won't you keep it out for my sake?' If you make one exception, of course, you're doomed. Everybody comes to you."

What Ed Sidey knows is that crime is not the big news in a small town. It's there, of course, but what counts to the people is life, the life they live day to day. Its high points are the births and the weddings . . . and the County Fair.

"Our news coverage is mostly picture coverage. And it's important to our readers that we get pictures of all those winners. Because if we don't, why some kid is hurt because he alone, of all the other beef champions, was not in the paper. So we make a great effort to catch every one. And we always miss one, but we always try next year to score a hundred percent."

The *Adair County Free Press* is not the *New York Times*. But, to the people of Greenfield, it's important. It matters in their lives.

"As long as I can remember, even as a kid working here on Wednesdays, and at that time it was the old letter-press operation and we used to print late at night—sometimes it was almost midnight—and still on a warm summer evening there would be a line of people standing outside, waiting for their paper. . . ."

Photo by TBS

A Slow Move into the Future

Iowa does not change quickly. It began as a farm state. It remains a farm state. In many places, the future is banging on the door, demanding to be let in, insisting that its time has come. In many places, the future presents an overwhelming challenge or a thrilling new possibility. In Iowa, the future will probably be a variation of the past.

Once the land was plowed with horses. Then it was plowed with tractors. Now, in some places, it is not plowed at all, but sprayed with chemicals in preparation for planting. It saves the topsoil. That's the kind of change that happens in Iowa. The old ways are given up when better ones have proved their worth.

But Iowa is unlikely to sprout high tech industries, sud-

A modern grain elevator.

denly, where soybeans used to grow.

Once the farm was the only source of income for most families. Then a few farmers and children of farmers began to take outside jobs. Today, 50 percent of all Iowa farmers are part-time farmers. A changing economy demands a change in lifestyle.

But Iowa is not going to stop feeding the nation in any future that we can foresee.

Once there was little manufacturing in Iowa. Then farm-related industry began to spring up. Today, there is a healthy balance between agriculture and manufacturing. In the future, the balance may tip away from farming.

But the most likely direction that manufacturing will take in Iowa is toward more processing of the food grown in the state. One foot will remain on the farm.

Change comes slowly in Iowa, slowly and carefully, the way corn is grown. The future grows out of the past.

RAGBRAI is an annual bicycle ride across Iowa. It is an event, a party, and a celebration of Iowa rolled all into one.

Important Historical Events in Iowa

1673 The first white men to visit the Iowa region are the French explorers Louis Joliet and Jacques Marquette.

1680 LaSalle sends Michel Aco and Father Louis Hennepin to explore the northern part of the Mississippi River. They pass by Iowa.

1690 Nicholas Perrot teaches the Indians how to mine lead. He sets up a trading post near present-day Dubuque.

1762 France gives Spain part of its lands west of the Mississippi, including Iowa.

1788 The Fox Indians give Julien Dubuque permission to mine lead in the area that is now Dubuque. He becomes the first white settler there.

1800 Spain secretly agrees to give back part of Louisiana, including Iowa, to France.

1803 Iowa becomes part of the United States as a result of the Louisiana Purchase.

1804-1806 Iowa is included in the Territory of Louisiana created by the U.S. government. Lewis and Clark explore the area. Zebulon Pike explores Iowa's Mississippi bluffs.

1808 Fort Madison is the first fort built in Iowa.

1812 Iowa becomes part of the Missouri Territory.

1813 Indians burn Fort Madison during the War of 1812.

1814 The Indians and the British defeat the Americans near Davenport.

1816 Fort Armstrong is established.

1831 The Sauk and Fox Indians are forced by the U.S. government to move from western Illinois into Iowa.

1832 Chief Black Hawk refuses to leave Illinois and goes to war with the United States. The Indians are defeated and give up their land.

1833 Permanent settlers move into the Iowa area.

1834 Iowa becomes part of the Michigan Territory.

1836 The U.S. government creates the Territory of Wisconsin, which includes Iowa.

1838 The Territory of Iowa is created on July 4 and includes all of what is now Iowa as well as parts of Minnesota and North and South Dakota. Robert Lucas is the first territorial governor. The capital is Burlington.

1841 The capital is moved to Iowa City.

1843 Fort Des Moines is built.

1846 Iowa is admitted to the Union as the 29th state on December 28. The governor is Ansel Briggs.

1847 The State University of Iowa is founded at Iowa City.

1856 The first bridge across the Mississippi River is built at Davenport.

1857 Iowa adopts its present constitution. The capital is moved to Des Moines.

1867 The first railroad in the state is completed. It runs from the Mississippi River to Council Bluffs.

1868 Iowa's first Grange Society is organized.

1873 Grange members gain control of the state legislature.

1874 The legislature enacts laws regulating freight rates in the state.

1878 The railroads are able to get the regulatory laws repealed.

1880 Farmers in Iowa switch from wheat to corn production.

1913 The Keokuk Dam is finished.

1918 Iowa farmland sells for record prices during and after World War I.

1920-1940 Farmers must take out large mortgages in order to pay for the expensive land. Many farmers lose their land through the Great Depression because they cannot pay the mortgages.

1952 The Mississippi and Missouri rivers overflow in huge floods.

1962 Iowa's court system is reorganized.

Mid-1970s Iowa's chief source of income shifts from agriculture to manufacturing.

Iowa Almanac

Nickname. The Hawkeye State.

Capital. Des Moines.

State Bird. Eastern Goldfinch.

State Flower. Wild Rose.

State Tree. Oak.

State Motto. Our liberties we prize and our rights we will maintain.

State Song. The Song of Iowa.

State Abbreviations. Ia. (traditional), IA (postal).

Statehood: December 28, 1846, the 29th state.

Government. Congress: U.S. senators, 2; U.S. representatives, 6. **State Legislature:** senators, 50; representatives, 100. **Counties:** 99.

Area. 56,290 sq. mi. (145,790 sq. km.), 25th in size among the states.

Greatest Distances. north/south, 210 mi. (338 km.); east/west, 324 mi. (521 km.).

Elevation. Highest: 1,670 ft. (509 m). **Lowest:** 480 ft. (146 m).

Population. 1980 Census: 2,913,387 (3% increase over 1970), 27th among the states. **Density:** 52 persons per sq. mi. (20 persons per sq. km.). **Distribution:** 59% urban, 41% rural. **1970 Census:** 2,825,368.

Economy. Agriculture: beef cattle, hogs, soybeans, corn, milk, eggs. **Manufacturing:** food products, electric and nonelectric machinery, chemicals, fabricated metal products, printed materials. **Mining:** stone, sand and gravel.

Places to Visit

Amana Colonies, near Cedar Rapids.
Dodge House in Council Bluffs.
Dvořák Memorial in Spillville.
Effigy Mounds National Monument, near McGregor.
Floyd Monument in Sioux City.
Grotto of Redemption in West Bend.
Little Brown Church, near Nashua.
Living History Farms, near Des Moines.

Annual Events

Estherville Winter Sports Festival (February).
Girls' and Boys' State Basketball Tournaments (March).
Tulip Festival in Orange City (May).
North Iowa Band Festival in Mason City (June).
Bix Beiderbecke Memorial Jazz Festival in Davenport (July).
Mesquakie Indian Powwow in Tama (August).
National Hot Air Balloon Races in Indianola (August).
Iowa State Fair in Des Moines (August).
Livestock Exposition in Waterloo (October).

Iowa Counties

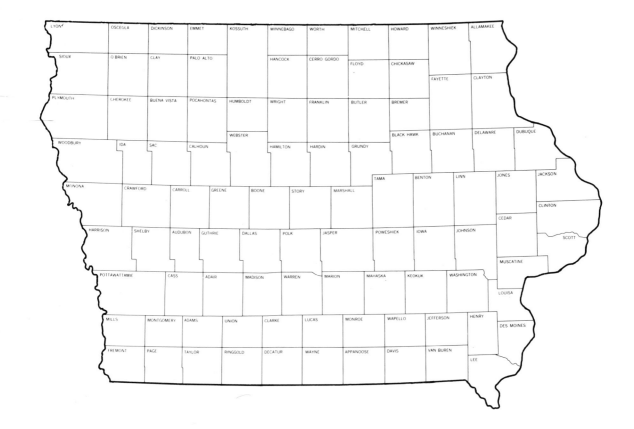

INDEX

architecture, 30

artists, 30-32, 35-36

Black Hawk Purchase, 14

Black Hawk War, 13

Bunyan, Paul, 23

cattle, 24, 25

Cavelier, Robert, 10

Civil War, 15

Clark, William, 12

corn, 7, 19, 23, 24, 26, 36, 44

County Fair, 41

culture (of Iowa), 34-37

Dubuque, 12

Dubuque, Julien, 10-11

economy (of Iowa), 22-27

education, 26-27

explorers, 10, 12

farming, 7, 10, 16, 18, 19, 21-27, 28, 29, 30, 43-44

food processing, 24, 44

future (of Iowa), 42-44

Glaspell, Susan, 35-36

Grange, 16

Great Depression, 19, 30

heart transplant, 28

history (of Iowa), 8-19, 45

hogs, 7, 19, 21, 24, 25, 28

Indians, 10, 11, 12, 13, 15

Irving, John, 36

Jefferson, Thomas, 11

John Deere Company, 24

Joliet, Louis, 10

landscape, 18, 31

La Salle, Sieur, 10

lead, 10-11

Lewis, Meriwether, 12

Lincoln, Abraham, 13

livestock, 25, 26

Louisiana Purchase, 11

lumber, 16-18

machinery, 24

manufacturing, 24-26, 44

Marquette, Jacques, 10

Miller, Glenn, 36

mining, 11

Mississippi River, 10, 16

Mississippi Valley, 10

Mound Builders, 9-10

music, 36

Napoléon, 11

neighbors, 7, 28-29

O'Connor, Flannery, 36

painting, 30-32

Perrot, Nicholas, 10

Pike, Zebulon, 12

playwright, 35

produce, 36

railroad, 15, 16, 18, 23

Sacagawea, 12

Santa Domingo, 11

schools, 7, 21, 26-27, 36

Sioux City, 12

Snodgrass, W.D., 36

soil, 7, 9, 24, 43

soybeans, 25, 44

statehood, 14-15

Territory of Iowa, 14

Territory of Michigan, 14

Territory of Missouri, 12

trading, 10, 12-13

University of Iowa, 36

veterinarian, 21

Wilson, Meredith, 36

Wisconsin Territory, 14

Wood, Grant, 30-32, 36